Melbourne has sof the reason why it is a city with a thrivi that blends cutting buildings that are a alleyways which house some of the world's best street art, the city's burgeoning bar scene and hundreds of restaurants and cafés.

CITIx60: Melbourne explores Australia's cultural and arts capital in five aspects, covering architecture, art spaces, shops and markets, eating and entertainment. With expert advice from 60 stars of the city's creative scene, this book guides you to the real attractions of the city for an authentic taste of Melbourne life.

Contents

Before You Go

BASIC INFO

Currency
Australian Dollar (AUD/S)
Exchange rate: US$1 : A$1.4

Time zone
GMT +10
DST +1

DST begins at 0200 (local time) on the first Sunday of October and ends at 0300 (local time) on the first Sunday of April.

Dialling
International calling: +61
Citywide: (0)3*

*Dial (0) for calls made within Australia.

Weather (avg. temperature range)
Spring (Sep-Nov): 10-22°C / 50-72°F
Summer (Dec-Feb): 13-25°C / 55-77°F
Autumn (Mar-May): 9-20°C / 48-68°F
Winter (Jun-Aug): 6-13°C / 43-55°F

USEFUL WEBSITES

Victoria's train, tram and bus timetables
www.metlinkmelbourne.com.au

Free public WiFi hotspots
www.visitvictoria.com/Information/WiFi-hotspots

EMERGENCY CALLS

Ambulance, fire or police
000

Consulates
China   +61 (0)3 9822 0604
France   +61 (0)3 9690 6075
Germany   +61 (0)3 9642 8088
Japan   +61 (0)3 9679 4510
Spain   +61 (0)3 9347 1966
UK   +61 (0)3 9652 1600
US   +61 (0)3 9526 5900

AIRPORT EXPRESS TRANSFER

Tullamarine Airport <-> Southern Cross Station (SkyBus)
Trains / Journey: every 10 mins / 20 mins
From Tullamarine Airport (T3) – 0010-2355 daily
From Southern Cross Station – 0000-2306 daily
One-way: $18 / Return: $36
www.skybus.com.au

Avalon Airport <-> Southern Cross Station (Airport Bus)
Trains / Journey: meet with every flight / 50 mins
One-way: $22 / Return: $42
www.sitacoaches.com.au

PUBLIC TRANSPORT IN MELBOURNE

Bus
Taxi
Train
Tram

Means of Payment
Credit cards
Cash
myk pass

GENERAL PUBLIC HOLIDAYS

January	1 New Year's Day, 26 Australia Day
March/April	Labour Day, Good Friday, Saturday before Easter Sunday, Easter Sunday & Monday, 25 ANZAC Day
June	13 Queen's Birthday
October	Friday before the AFL Grand Final
November	Melbourne Cup
December	25 Christmas Day, 26 Boxing Day

Museums and galleries here normally open on public holidays, except during Good Friday and Christmas.

FESTIVALS / EVENTS

February
White Night Melbourne
whitenightmelbourne.com.au
St. Jerome's Laneway Festival
melbourne.lanewayfestival.com
Supergraph (or March)
www.supergraph.com.au

March
Virgin Australia Melbourne Fashion Festival
www.vamff.com.au

April
Melbourne International Design Week (or May)
www.designmattersvictoria.com/design-week

May
Next Wave (Biannual)
nextwave.org.au

July
Open House Melbourne
www.openhousemelbourne.org

August
Melbourne International Film Festival
(through to September)
miff.com.au
Melbourne Art Fair
melbourneartfair.com.au
Craft Cubed Festival
craftcubed.org.au

September
Melbourne Fringe Festival
www.melbournefringe.com.au

October
Melbourne Festival
www.festival.melbourne

December
Stereosonic
stereosonic.com.au

Event days vary by year. Please check for
updates online.

UNUSUAL OUTINGS

Melbourne Street Art Tours
www.melbournestreettours.com

Hot Air Balloon Ride
www.balloonman.com.au

Rap Jumping
rapjumping.com

Great Ocean Road Tour
greatoceanroadmelbournetours.com.au

The Old Melbourne Gaol Night Tour
www.oldmelbournegaol.com.au

SMARTPHONE APP

Journey planner
Public Transport Victoria

Free bikers' map
Spotcycle

Restaurant reviewed by locals
Zomato

REGULAR EXPENSES

A regular donut
$0.8-1

Domestic / International mail (postcards)
$1.40/1.95-2.75

Gratuities
Tipping is not necessary in Australia.
On licensed taxis: Round up to the nearest
dollar.

Count to 10

What makes Melbourne so special?

Illustrations by Guillaume Kashima aka Funny Fun

Life in Melbourne is a rich multicultural blend of the many different cultures, festivals, cuisines and music of the city's diverse inhabitants. This is a city overflowing with artistic and creative thinkers, which is expressed in every facet of everyday Melbourne life. Whether you are on a one-day stopover or a week-long stay, see what Melbourne's creatives consider essential to see, taste, read and take home from your trip.

1

Architecture

**Domed Building,
State Library of Victoria**
by Bates, Pebbles & Smart

Cairo Flats
by Acheson Best Overend

Arts Centre Melbourne Spire
by Roy Grounds

Manchester Unity Building (#6)
by Marcus R. Barlow

Burnham Beeches
by Harry A Norris

Olympic Swimming Stadium
by Kevin Borland, Peter McIntyre,
J and P Murphy

Shrine of Rememberance
updated by Ashton Raggatt
McDougall, Rush Wright & Associates

5

Specialty Coffee House & Roasters

NOLA Iced Coffee
ChungKing Express (1994)
www.everyday-coffee.com

Standing room café in the subway
Cup Of Truth
FB: Cup Of Truth

Magic Coffee
Dukes Coffee Roasters
www.dukescoffee.com.au

Coffee, music & design
Brother Baba Budan
www.brotherbababudan.com.au

Coffee house in an old converted horse stable
The Virtue of the Coffee Drink
vertuecoffee.com.au

Coffee roastery & retailer
Market Lane
marketlane.com.au

6

Breakfast & Brunch Spots

Japanese-style in a backstreet warehouse
Cibi Café
cibi.com.au

Beautifully crafted brunch
Top Paddock café
toppaddockcafe.com

Quaint little cafe
Twenty and Six
www.twentyandsix.com.au

Thai breakfast & Beci Orpin menu
Magic Mountain Saloon
magicmountainsaloon.com.au

Seasonal breakfast in a beautiful warehouse
East Elevation
eastelevation.com.au

Bircher muesli with the dehydrated mandarin
Wide Open Road
wideopenroad.com.au

7

Pastries

Pork roll
N.Lee Bakery
220 Smith St., Collingwood

Salted caramel donut
Cobb Lane
www.cobblane.com.au

Doughnuts filled with hot jam
Olympic Doughnuts
Footscray train station

Custard doughnuts
Baker D. Chirico
bakerdchirico.com.au

Cheese pies
Al Bakery
Sydney Rd., Brunswick

Waffle & baguettes
Waffle On
FB: WaffleOn.Melbourne

8

Street Art Hunting

Original Banksy art
Revolver Upstairs
revolverupstairs.com.au

Hosier & Rutledge Lane
opposite Federation Square

Caledonian Lane
off Little Bourke St.

Union Lane
off Bourke Street Mall

Flinders Lane
corner of Cocker Alley

Carlton
122 Palmerston St.

Centre Place
*between Collins St. &
Flinders Ln.*

ACDC Lane
between Exhibition St. & Russell St.

9

Rooftop Bars

Naked in the Sky
www.nakedforsatan.com.au/naked-
in-the-sky

Bomba (#50)
www.bombabar.com.au

Siglo
www.facebook.com/SigloBar

Madame Brussels
www.madamebrussels.com

Wolf's Lair
jimmywatsons.com/wolfs-lair

Rooftop Bar @Curtain House (#22)
(Seasonal)
rooftopcinema.com.au

Goldilocks
www.goldilocksbar.com.au

Loop Roof
www.looprooftopbar.com.au

10

Live Music & Gig Venues

Some Velvet Morning
somevelvetmorning.com.au

Standard Hotel in Fitzroy
www.thestandardhotel.com.au

The Retreat in Brunswick
retreathotelbrunswick.com.au

Bennetts Land
www.bennettslane.com

The Spotted Mallard
www.spottedmallard.com

The Cornet Hotel
cornerhotel.com

Forum Melbourne (#7)
www.forummelbourne.com.au

The Toff in Town (#59)
www.thetoffintown.com

Icon Index

 Opening hours   Admission

 Address   Facebook

 Contact   Website

 Remarks

 Scan QR codes to access Google Maps and discover the area around each destination. Internet connection required.

60x60

60 Local Creatives x 60 Hotspots

From street art filled laneways to a rich blend of foods from all corners of the world, there is much to inspire creative urges in Melbourne. 60x60 points you to 60 haunts where 60 arbiters of taste develop their nose for the good stuff.

Landmarks & Architecture · SPOTS · 01 – 12

Experience contemporary buildings, grungy graffiti clad laneways and beautiful green open spaces. Start at Federation Square and meander through to Melbourne University.

Cultural & Art Spaces · SPOTS · 13 – 24

Be spoilt for choice with theatre, comedy, street art, dance, ballet, musicals, indigenous art, sculpture, contemporary or classical art and much more happening every day.

Markets & Shops · SPOTS · 25 – 36

Get lost trawling through unique gift and souvenir stores, earthy markets, high end fashion stores, cute little pottery stores and everything in between.

Restaurants & Cafés · SPOTS · 37 – 48

Start your day with breakfast at Auction Rooms and stroll through the laneways stopping for coffee or a drink at the many rooftop bars. End with a glass of wine at Cumulus Up.

Nightlife · SPOTS · 49 – 60

Enjoy sunset cocktails and a bite to eat on one of many rooftop bars, before going on a bar crawl through the city's laneways taking in live music, DJs, jazz and comedians.

Landmarks & Architecture

Historic architecture, cultural precincts and super stage of sports

The architecture of Melbourne is a beautiful blend of new contemporary buildings, open public spaces, abstract architecture (#3) and old neo-gothic buildings (#6), often with street art filled laneways weaving around at their bases. While North Melbourne's many perfectly maintained Victorian buildings provide a glimpse into the city's elegant past, a walk along the Yarra River through the ritzy suburbs of Toorak, South Yarra and Hawthorn will show some of the amazing Tudor, Tudorbethan, Georgian and Victorian mansions built following Melbourne's gold rush during the mid 1800s. To the north of the neatly gridded CBD find a snapshot of Melbourne's industrial past. The inner city suburbs of Fitzroy, Collingwood and Abbotsford were gentrified in the 1980s and 1990s. The surge in rent prices in these areas forced out much of the manufacturing industries but magnetised a band of hipsters to re-energise the abandoned warehouses with reviving brews and creative forces. Melbourne's city life is well-balanced by abundant perfectly manicured gardens and huge green parks, such as The Royal Botanic Gardens, and sportsground such as the MCG (#4), Rod Laver Arena (where the annual Australian Open is played) and AAMI Park. With a relatively flat ground, Melbourne is best explored by bike or rides on the famously convenient tram lines. For a breathtaking panorama of the city, check out the Edge (www.eurekaskydeck.com.au). The four-sided glass cube commands a truly encompassing views from Melbourne's tallest building, the Eureka Tower in the Southbank.

Studio Constantine
Communication design studio

We are Hannah and David Constantine of Studio Constantine. Everything we do and make is committed to being beautiful, articulate, incisive, relevant to our client's and their market.

NGV International P.014

University of Melbourne P.016

Archier
Design studio

Composed of architects Chris Haddad, Josh FitzGerald and Chris Gilbert with Victorian and Tasmanian roots, Archier creates elegantly minimal architecture, furniture and lighting.

Jake Stollery
Illustrator

Jake Stollery's work intersects the lines between fashion, art and technology. It draws inspiration from a mix of 90s cyberpunk, dusty science fiction and new media experiments.

Federation Square P.018

Tim Sutherland
Creative director, StudioBrave

Tim Sutherland is the founder and creative director of StudioBrave, a creative agency devoted to unique and distinctive brand design.

Melbourne Cricket Ground P.019

Carlton Gardens P.020

Tim White
Director

Tim White is a commercial and music video director who spends half his time in Melbourne and the other half working abroad. His clients include Honda and the City of Tokyo.

Michael Drescher
Associate director, DKO

I am an architect and interior designer. I have been captivated by Melbourne's many unique layers since moving here ten years ago. As a lover of food and design, this city is perfect.

Manchester Unity Building P.022

Simone Speet & Emma Holder, *Büro North*

Büro North designers Simone is originally from Sydney and Emma an ex-Wellingtonian. They both moved to Melbourne to experience its cultural, creative and sporting atmosphere.

Abbotsford Convent
P.024

Alexandra Kovac
Fashion designer

I run a boutique womenswear label called Oracles. I also DJ in a duo called Rainbow Connection. We play fun boogie and disco music around town.

Juliet Burnett
Dancer

I'm a ballet dancer, writer, human and animal rights and environmental activist. I was a senior artist at The Australian Ballet and will now continue my dancing career overseas.

Forum Melbourne
P.023

Fitzroy backstreets
P.026

Hanna Richardson & Katherine Kemp, *ZWEI*

ZWEI is an architectural and interior practice that believes in the creation of authentic, sensory experiential spaces with a strong narrative and a sense of personality.

Moonee Ponds Creek Trail
P.028

Pandarosa
Creative studio

Pandarosa is made up of Ariel and Andii. Our main objective is to give the mundane wall, brochure or inanimate object life, blood and a heart.

Phil Ferguson
Artist

I mainly create crocheted hats and post them on Instagram as @chiliphilly, an account I started to make new friends after I moved to Melbourne from Perth.

Nicholas Building
P.027

Our Magic Hour
P.029

1 NGV International
Map D, P.105

The custodian of a trove of important art from Europe, Asia, America, and Oceania, NGV International's architecture by key Modernist figure Sir Roy Grounds (1905-81) is as mesmer- izing as its blockbuster exhibitions. The original exterior and recent interior remodelling by Mario Bellini are outstanding in their own right, however the star of the show is the Leonard French stained glass ceiling in the Great Hall – one of the world's largest pieces of suspended stained glass. Spend a Friday night at the NGV for live performances and after-hour access to exhibitions next to pop-up talks and great food.

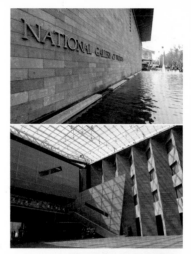

🕐 1000-1700 daily   🏠 180 St Kilda Rd., Southbank
📞 +61 (0)3 8620 2222   🔗 www.ngv.vic.gov.au
📎 Only ground level exhibitions open on Tuesdays

"One of our favourite haunts is the gallery containing the collection of Mesoamerican sculpture and decorative arts."

– Hannah & David Constantine, Studio Constantine

2 University of Melbourne
Map H, P.107

Founded in 1853, the University of Melbourne is Australia's second oldest university and boasts an aesthetically pleasing blend of period architecture and contemporary designs. Amongst the latest additions is the Faculty of Architecture, Building and Planning building jointly done by John Wardle Architects and NADAAA. The South Lawn Underground Car Park, which was built in 1972 is Australia's first fully enclosed and concealed subterrestrial landscape, featuring a forest of concrete columns integrating downpipes as a stormwater runoff system design. A scene from the original Mad Max film was also filmed here.

🏠 Grattan St., Parkville
📞 +61 (0)3 9035 5511
URL www.unimelb.edu.au

"Our favourite part of the university is the South Lawn Underground Car Park, which looks like a cross between a vast Gothic crypt and a dystopian cityscape."

– Chris Haddad, Josh FitzGerald & Chris Gilbert, Archier

3　Federation Square
Map B, P.105

Federation Square, or "Fed Square" as locals call it, is Melbourne's cultural epicentre. Occupying a prime position next to the Yarra River, Botanic Gardens and Flinders Street Station, the 3.8 hectares of space exerts a system of spatial and surface geometries, designed by LAB Architecture and local firm Bates Smart, that allows for individual buildings at the square to stand out on their own while uniting as a visual whole, with the use of only three cladding materials: sandstone, glass and zinc. Stop by for progressive programmes in the main public space or at ACMI.

🕐 ACMI: 1000-1700 daily
🏠 Corner Swanston & Flinders St., CBD　📞 + 61 (0)3 9655 1900
URL www.fedsquare.com

"*The architecture's complexity and details still blow my mind every time I see it. Also, it's right next to Hosier Lane with constantly evolving street art.*"
– Jake Stollery

4 Melbourne Cricket Ground
Map C, P.105

Built in 1853, less than 20 years after Melbourne was founded, the MCG is a spiritual place for Melburnian sports lovers and dubbed by this Aussie rules football obsessed city its "beating heart". It's been the home of Aussie rules football since 1859, and was the birthplace of Test cricket in 1877, one-day international cricket in 1971 and the main stadium for the 1956 Olympic Games and 2006 Commonwealth Games. Architecturally it has historical signifi-

cance aligned with its beautiful contemporary updates. On a non-event day, book a guided tour to explore the inner sanctum of the MCG and Australian sporting heritage at the National Sports Museum.

🕐 *Opening hours vary with event*
🏠 *Brunton Ave., Richmond*
📞 *+61 (0)3 9657 8888*
🔗 *www.mcg.org.au*

"Go with a local to an AFL game so they can explain it. And go to a blockbuster like the Anzac Day game Collingwood v Essendon. Finals are also spectacular."

– Tim Sutherland, StudioBrave

5 Carlton Gardens & Royal Exhibition Building
Map A, P.102

Erected for the 1880 Melbourne International Exhibition, listed as a World Heritage Site, Carlton Gardens and Royal Exhibition Building enjoy a plum position between the CBD, Carlton and Fitzroy. The northern section of the park holds the Museum, tennis courts and a children's playground designed as a Victorian maze, while the southern section harbours picturesque duck ponds and a big fountain. The Exhibition Building at the centre is a meld of the Byzantine, Romanesque, Lombardic and Italian Renaissance styles designed by Joseph Reed and looks especially impressive at night.

🏠 1-111 Carlton St., Carlton
🖉 Royal Exhibition Building: Only opens in times of exhibition. Guided tours: 1400 daily, $10/8/7, museumvictoria.com.au/reb

"I personally prefer the southern half of the Gardens as it gets more sunlight in the later hours of the day."
– Tim White

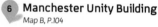

6 Manchester Unity Building

Map B, P.104

Melbourne's iconic Manchester Unity Building is a neo-Gothic building completed in 1932. Its architecture and materiality beautifully engage this dominant city corner which is as beautiful by day as it is by night. The construction speed itself was a remarkable human feat, so as the design. The massive use of steel and marble, mother-of-pearl coloured glazed terracotta (or faience) tiles, and large plate-glass windows was a bold gesture to reinvigorate a city shackled by economic depression. It is usually open to the public during 'Melbourne open house', so mark your calendar.

🏠 107 Swanston St., CBD
URL www.manchesterunitybuilding.com.au 🖉 Guided tours by Open House Melbourne: www.openhousemelbourne.org

"The way materials meet and interact with each other is inspiring. Keep an eye out for the six-metre original boardroom table that has survived all the building's refurbishments."

– Michael Drescher, DKO

7 Forum Melbourne
Map B, P.105

Formerly Melbourne's State Theatre, the Forum is one of the city's most readily identified landmarks. Its Gothic statues and perhaps exaggerated arabic-inspired architecture has cut an impressive figure into Melbourne's skyline since 1929 and its amazing sound system and incredible interior makes for a wonderful venue to take in a wide array of live entertainment acts and concerts. On your visit, make sure you look for the reproductions of Greco-Roman statuary and up at the sky-blue ceiling decorated with small stars that create a twilight sky effect. Book tickets to shows well in advance as they sell out quickly.

🕐 *Opening hours & admission vary with programmes*
🏠 *154 Flinders St., CBD*
URL *www.forummelbourne.com.au, www.ticketmaster.com.au*

"With a pumping sound system and impressive architecture inside and out, the Forum is the best place to experience local and international theatre and music."
– Simone Speet & Emma Holder, Büro North

8 Abbotsford Convent
Map N, P.109

With a history dating back to 1842, the Abbotsford Convent has evolved from a politician's home to a convent and then to the community hub that it is today. Only about 15 minutes away from the CBD by bicycle, the Convent is a perfect union of countryside vibe and convenient location, with an extensive programme of events staged throughout the year for every age. Drop into Collingwood Children's farm and café for delicious fresh produce or hit up the community run restaurant Lentil As Anything for great vegetarian food. In the summer there are night markets with food, parties and outdoor screenings at The Shadow Electric.

🕐 0730–2200 daily
🏠 1 St Heliers St., Abbotsford
📞 +61 (0)3 9415 3600
🔗 abbotsfordconvent.com.au

"*Make sure you take a walk along the Yarra trail to Dights Falls and back – it's magic!*"

– Alexandra Kovac, Oracles

9 Fitzroy backstreets
Map A, P.102

Fitzroy, Melbourne's first suburb created in 1839, has been long associated with the working class and is currently home to a wide variety of ethnicities and socio-economic groups. These days it also provides an evolving outdoor gallery of street art. Take a walk around the backstreets between Brunswick, Smith, Gertrude and Johnston Streets and you'll find yourself surrounded by spray-paint graffiti, murals and stencil art created by local and international artists. The area also boasts an eclectic mix of architecture ranging from bluestone miner's cottages to iron-lace bedecked terraces and rustic warehouses. Get your camera ready.

🏠 Backstreets between Brunswick, Smith, Gertrude and Johnston St., Fitzroy

"Let yourself get lost, and walk down every tiny laneway and tree lined street you come across to see the best street art."

– Juliet Burnett

10 Nicholas Building
Map B, P.104

Designed by architect Harry Norris (1888–1966), the Nicholas Building captures the creative heart of Melbourne. Originally built as part of the thriving Flinders Lane garment trade in 1926, the space is now divided into studios used by artists, designers and makers alike. Influenced by the 'Chicago Style', the architecture consists of nine floors with a grey terracotta faience façade manufactured as 'Granitex' by Wunderlich. The exterior has signs of a Greek revival style in its façade treatment, which uses ionic pilasters to divide the upper façade into bays and giant ordered columns define the building's lower half.

🏠 *37 Swanston St., CBD*
URL *thenicholasbuilding.blogspot. com.au*

"Enter through the old lift and wander the halls and look into the various studios. If you go to a regular Open Studio event you can purchase directly from the artist."
– Hanna Richardson & Katherine Kemp, ZWEI

11 Moonee Ponds Creek Trail
Map R, P.110

Running through urban Melbourne, with a part of it stretching alongside and underneath the CityLink, the Moonee Ponds Creek Trail provides a unique view into the underbelly of the inner city freeway. Depart from Docklands and head north to Brunswick West, you will encounter a number of concrete storm drains that have been used as a canal for coal barges, realigned and concreted in the 1950s and 2000s to keep the city away from floods. Recent habitat conservation work has brought about native trees and pobblebonk frogs and nankeen night heron alike in the upper catchment, best to be enjoyed either by foot or by riding a bike.

🏠 *Docklands Dr., Docklands to Hope St., Brunswick West*

"*Always look up, it really helps in getting a sense of scale and placement about the bizarreness of this location, although doing this while riding might be tricky.*"

– Ariel & Andii, Pandarosa

12 Our Magic Hour
Map G, P.107

Mounted atop a clump of industrial buildings at Cremorne, Our Magic Hour was created by Swiss-born mixed media artist Ugo Rondinone whose installations are frequently constructed to encourage shifting moods. Commissioned by Kaldor Public Art Projects and first exposed to the public at his solo exhibition in 2003 on the roof of the Museum of Contemporary Art in Sydney, the rainbow-hued neon sign hinted at his carnival figures at the show and, like a down-turned smile, its melancholy ambience. Best views are from across the river, approximately where Caroline Street and Alexandra Avenue converge.

🏠 11 Palmer Parade, Cremorne

"It's such a nice thing to see when you walk along Alexandra Ave. Make sure you see it at night. It doesn't look as cool if you see it during the day."

– Phil Ferguson

Cultural & Art Spaces

Housemuseums, revered cinemas and carbon-neutral crafts

Melbourne's culture and arts scene is a diverse, vibrant, fun and interesting mix of festivals, exhibitions and live entertainment gigs, which offers everything from musicals, plays, theatre, concerts, ballet and comedy shows in the city's many live entertainment venues, to contemporary, classical, indigenous art, craft and sculpture exhibitions in the more than 100 galleries peppered throughout the city and suburbs. Melbourne has some beautiful leafy outdoor venues such as Heide (#13) and The Abbotsford Convent (#8) and also some urban outdoor venues such as Rooftop Bar and Cinema (#22). The city also seems to have at least one festival happening every day such as the world famous Melbourne International Comedy Festival, the Melbourne International Film Festival, and Midsumma Festival, amongst the countless food, wine and cultural festivals. Many of the suburbs have their own street party festivals also – the biggest is the St Kilda Festival in February, which attracts more than 250,000 people each year to watch the many free concerts along the beach, DJs playing in bars, clubs and at the many street parties along Fitzroy and Acland Streets. Go to *www.melbournefestivals.com.au* to find what festivals are happening when you are in town. If you decide to head down the picturesque Great Ocean Road, make sure you pay a visit to Qdos (*www.qdos-arts.com*). The Lorne site has a spectacular sculpture gallery in the forest and a small indoor gallery behind the café.

Paris Thomson
Founder, SIRAP

Born and bred in Melbourne and travelling the world often with camera in hand, Paris is a film director with a love for wine, cheese and considered design.

Lyon House-museum P.036

Virginia Martin
Fashion designer

I'm the owner and designer of the womenswear label, búl. I focus on minimalistic yet classic shapes, easy-to-wear relaxing fit and luxe fabrics.

Laura Phillips
Editor, Open Journal

A Melbourne native, Laura Phillips founded Mr. Wolf Magazine, a journal of nordic design, and is now the editor of Open Journal, a publication on architecture, urbanism and design.

Heide Museum of Modern Art P.034

Robin Boyd Foundation P.037

Ben Grosz & Laura Camilleri, *Grosz Co.Lab*

When not running their design consultancy, the pair travel the world on design led excursions to continue inspiring their diverse creative practice.

Daine Singer P.040

Antonia Sellbach
Artist & musician

Antonia Sellbach is known for her large scale abstract paintings. She is also a musician with local bands Love of Diagrams and Beaches and co-founded feminist project, LISTEN.

Alice Oehr
Designer & illustrator

I am a designer and illustrator living in Melbourne with my sister and my cat. I love to go out and soak up the atmosphere of Melbourne - there is always something on.

ACCA P.038

Craft Victoria P.041

Beci Orpin
Designer, illustrator & author

I have released three DIY books and in 2015, my first children's book. I live in Melbourne with my husband Raph, sons Tyke and Ari and two British shorthair cats Tio and Miso.

Mikala Tai
Curator, Supergraph

I mainly work on contemporary art, fashion and also run Supergraph, Melbourne's contemporary graphic art fair. I believe good design makes every day a little more special.

Abigail Crompton
Director, Third Drawer Down

I am a director of a product design studio, a wholesaler and a retailer. I collaborate with artists and museums worldwide focusing on the challenges posed by cultural retailing.

Bliss & Bonnie Adams
Founders, Marble Basics

We are sisters born and bred in Melbourne. We design marble homewares for our label Marble Basics. Our designs are functional, timeless and we pride them on simplicity.

Tooth and Claw
Video production house

Tooth and Claw is a boutique video production company specialising in musically driven video works. We love what we do and we play well with others.

Lola Berry
Nutritionist

I'm a nutritionist, author and yogi nerd. I work in media writing and also talk on radio and TV about health and loving every second of it. I'm all about living the best life you can.

13 Heide Museum of Modern Art

Map T, P.110

A well worth 20-minute drive from the CBD will take you to the Heide Museum of Modern Art, where John and Sunday Reed used to live and receive artists, writers and intellectuals. The couple were noted for their relentless support of Australian art. As their art collection outgrew their first residence (Heide I), the couple commissioned a second home (Heide II) in 1964, as a "gallery to be lived in". Since it opened its door to the public in 1981, the Heide remains a temple for modern and contemporary art and a popular destination to escape the city grind. Allow a good two to three hours to take everything in.

🕐 1000–1700 (Tu–Su), Café Vue: 1000–1700 (Tu–F), 0900– (Sa–Su)
💲 $16/14/12
🏠 7 Templestowe Rd., Bulleen
📞 +61 (0)3 9850 1500
URL www.heide.com.au
🔗 Free guided tours: 1400 (Tu–Su)

"Top your trip off with settling into a long lunch at Café Vue. Grab an uber for the drive there and back if you're planning to settle into a few drinks!"
– Paris Thomson, SIRAP

035

14 Lyon Housemuseum
Map U, P.110

Cross the threshold of Lyon Housemuseum and you'll also be at Corbett and Yueji Lyon's residence. Citing influences from a lineage of private collections in domestic settings, such as New York's Frick Collection, the Peggy Guggenheim Collection in Venice or, more locally, Heide (#13), Corbett Lyon, an architect and art collector himself, designed this large double height complex where friends and the public can view paintings, sculpture, video work and installations by the likes of Howard Arkley, Patricia Piccinini and Shaun Gladwel. Expect to experience art space and living space at once wherever you go.

⏱ By appointment only 💲 $22 (guided tour incl.)
🏠 219 Cotham Rd., Kew
📞 +61 (0)3 9817 2300
URL www.lyonhousemuseum.com.au

"The juxtaposition of walking through their well designed kitchen and looking at superb art, brings home that art is something to be lived in and surrounded by in daily life."

– Virginia Martin, búl

036

15 Robin Boyd Foundation

Map G, P.107

Established in 2005 and built upon Robin Boyd's (1919-1971) compelling life and long-running dedication to progressing the International Modern Movement in the Australian architectural scene, Robin Boyd Foundation organises expansive learning programmes to provide a rare insight into Australia's mid-century cultural shift. Programmes include public open days, forums and performances, and take place at Walsh Street, the South Yarra house which Boyd designed for his family and gave the architect a prominence in 1958. Take in the benefits of good design as you enter the house.

🏠 290 Walsh St., South Yarra
📞 +61 (0)3 9820 9838 URL www.robinboyd.org.au
🔗 Afternoon teas & twilight drinks: $45, bookings required

"Visits can be arranged via afternoon teas or twilight drinks."

– Laura Phillips, Open Journal

16 ACCA
Map D, P.105

A bold rusted form, clad in a singular rusty steel façade, the ACCA building was developed by local architects Wood Marsh in 2002 as 'a sculpture in which to show art'. Based on the European model of the Kunsthalle, ACCA is now one of Melbourne's leading contemporary art spaces that bring the latest and most significant artwork by living artists from around the world for free to Melbourne audiences. Dubbed the "Yellow Peril", Vault, the steel plate sculpture by Ron Robertson-Swann outside ACCA, has been seriously mooted and on the move since it was unveiled in 1980 and finally settled in its current spot.

⏰ 1000-1700 (Tu-F), 1200- (Sa-Su)
🏠 111 Sturt St., Southbank
☎ +61 (0)3 9697 9999
🔗 www.accaonline.org.au

"The building and the ever-changing work that it houses are well worth a visit."

– Ben Grosz & Laura Camilleri, Grosz Co.Lab

 Daine Singer
Map B, P.104

At the heart of the restaurants and galleries lining Flinders Lane you'll find independent curator Daine Singer's gallery down in Customs House's basement, which she lent her name to also. Previously a gallery manager at the reputable Anna Schwartz Gallery on the same strip and curator at the NGV, Singer is widely recognised as one of the new young bloods in the city's commercial sphere and represents a circle of Australian contemporary artists, including Minna Gilligan, Zoë Croggon and Andrew McQualter. Past exhibitions have projected a careful balance between boundary pushing experimental art and more commercial work across mediums.

🕐 1200–1700 (W–F), –1600 (Sa)
🏠 Basement, 325 Flinders Ln., CBD
📞 +61 (0)410 264 036
🌐 www.dainesinger.com

"It's one of Melbourne's best galleries filled with cutting edge work by both emerging and established artists."

– Antonia Sellbach

18 Craft Victoria
Map B, P.105

Descend a few steps from Flinders Lane and you'll reach Craft Victoria's galleries where exhibitions rotate approximately every six weeks. A non-profit backed by a friendly team of staff who are all artists themselves, Craft represents the flower of contemporary Victorian ceramicists, jewellery makers, glassblowers, weavers and woodworkers and regularly demonstrates new ideas and techniques in traditional crafts. This place also houses a library and retail space full of inspiring work. Craft Cubed is an annual month-long festival which entails over satellite events, workshops, talks and open studios, all about crafts.

🕐 1100-1800 (M-Sa except P.H.)
🏠 31 Flinders Ln., CBD
📞 +61 (0)3 9650 7775
URL www.craft.org.au

"Wander into this great place to buy something that's really beautiful, totally unique and locally made."
–Alice Oehr

19 Lamington Drive

Map A, P.103

Pop in on both The Jacky Winter Group's head-quarters and the independent agency's exhibition room in one go. Since 2008, Lamington Drive has established itself as a gallery space where representing commercial cartoonists, photographers, artists and designers from all walks of life showcase their art. Try to align your visit with an exhibition opening night which usually fall on Wednesdays from 6-9pm and always include lamingtons (a traditional Australian dessert), refreshing beverages and good conversation.

🕐 1100-1800 (W-F), 1200-1700 (Sa)
🏠 101A Sackville St., Collingwood
📞 +61 (0)3 8060 9745
URL *lamingtondrive.com*

"Check when they have openings – they are usually a fun night when they are on. Also artworks here are often edition based and quite affordable."

– Beci Orpin

20 BUS Projects
Map A, P.103

With a revolving roster of excellent shows, this artist-run initiative is a great pulse check of the city's artistic beat. Beginning in 2001 as a design collective and a project space, BUS now promotes and collaborates with quite a few Australian artists across a wide range of mediums. Located at a former mid-20th century paint factory, which was re-designed by John Wardle Architects who work next door, BUS also operates outside of traditional gallery contexts, developing exhibitions, events, and performances off-site. Both their website and facebook show regular programme updates.

🕙 1200–1800 (Tu-F), 1000–1600 (Sa)
🏠 25-31 Rokeby St., Collingwood
☎ +61 (0)3 9995 8359
🔗 www.busprojects.org.au

"he café next door provides you with a great coffee hit!"

– Mikala Tai, Supergraph

21 Bennetts Lane Jazz Club
Map B, P.104

Bennetts Lane Jazz Club is an iconic Melbourne music institution. The intimate club has been showcasing the best local and international jazz and big band acts nightly for more than 20 years. Bennetts Lane hosts gigs all year round and is a venue of the Melbourne International Jazz Festival held annually from late May to early June. Past lineups have seen Justin Timberlake, Wynton Marsalis, Prince, Chick Corea and Kurt Elling to mention just a few. The club is likely to move out of its current location in early 2016 and bring their gigs to Flinders Lane mid-year, do check their website for updates.

🕐 *Opening hours & admission vary with programme*
🏠 *25 Bennetts Ln., CBD, June 2016: 136 Flinders Ln., CBD*
📞 *+61 (0)3 9663 2856*
URL *www.bennettslane.com*

"It is advisable not to talk while the band is playing as people take the shows seriously."

– Abigail Crompton, Third Drawer Down

22 Rooftop Cinema @Curtin House

Map B, P.104

Rooftop Cinema is a much loved Melbourne open air cinema atop of Curtin House on Swanston Street, right in the heart of the CBD. As the name suggests, the cinema is nestled on the building's rooftop which has been fitted out with deckchairs and a projector that shows a diverse range of films from art house and classic 80s to recent thrillers and dramas. The Rooftop Bar is also open from midday to serve you a cheeky drink or two before the film. Tickets are roughly $20 and, even in summer, it can get pretty chilly so it is best to have some warm clothes on hand.

🕐 Dec-Apr: Mid-day to 0100 daily
🏠 Curtin House, 252 Swanston St., CBD
URL www.rooftopcinema.com.au
f Rooftop Cinema

"It's the best way to soak in Melbourne's skyline, go at sunset and get there early to get the best seats. Head downstairs to Cookie after for delicious modern Thai."

– Bliss & Bonnie Adams, Marble Basics

23 The Astor Theatre
Map P, P.109

Long famous for its repertory programme and collection of classic, modern and cult movies, The Astor Theatre is a grand historic art-deco cinema with stalls and a dress circle that opened its doors in 1936. It is the last single screen cinema of its kind in continuous operation in Melbourne and one of only a few left operating in the world. The only part of the Astor that isn't old fashioned is its state-of-the-art sound system and giant screen. Pick any movie from their calendar for an engrossing movie experience at their magnificent 1,150 seat auditorium. Only selected screenings accept pre-bookings online.

🕐 Opens an hour prior to show (W-M)
💲 Ticket price varies with programmes
🏠 Corner Chapel St. & Dandenong Rd., St Kilda
📞 +61 (0)3 9510 1414 URL www.astortheatre.net.au

"The cream of Melbourne cinemas – it has been saved from closure many times by local cinefiles. Check out the website well in advance."

– Tooth and Claw

24 St Kilda Twilight Market
Map L, P.108

The St Kilda Twilight Market brings the community together on Thursday evenings in summer in a beautiful location, beneath palm trees and the twinkling stars beside Luna Park and the beach. The markets are filled with stalls selling a wonderful array of artworks, vintage wear, craft, hand designed fashion and jewellery, exotic clothes and foods of the world. The best way to get there is to walk, ride a bike or take the tram – the 96, 16, 3/3a and 79 trams will all get you there.

🕐 Dec–Feb: 1700–2200 (Th)
🏠 O'Donnell Gardens, St Kilda
📞 +61 (0)403 119 998
URL stkildatwilightmarket.com

"This is super rustic and has such a great vibe. Added bonus: brilliant food. Get there in time to watch the sunset, it's pretty special."
– Lola Berry

Markets & Shops

Homegrown labels, curated lifestyle products and weekend markets

Shopping, shopping, shopping and more shopping....there are so many amazing boutiques, stores and markets spread out across Melbourne. From the culinary delights, farmers market and souvenir stalls of the Queen Victoria Market in the CBD, the trash and treasure and handmade crafts of the Camberwell Sunday Market (#35) to the earthy St Andrews Market (#36) in Melbourne's bushy outskirts you'll be spoilt for choice and be able to have a very different experience at one of the numerous markets. If you love fashion and jewellry make sure you check out the small boutiques such as Lucy Folk Jewellery (#32) or Incu (#26). Bargain clothing hunters will love DFO in Docklands (www.dfo.com.au/SouthWharf) and for any hipsters there is a wide range of vintage clothing stores in Brunswick and Fitzroy. If you're in Fitzroy make sure you check out Third Drawer Down (#25) for unique art and design products. Other shopping strips that are brimming with stores are the stretch of Chapel Street between Toorak and Dandenong Roads. It starts with commercial brands, such as Providence Clothing Store, DKNY and Scanlan Theodore near Toorak Road and between High Street toward Dandenong Road there are lots of independent designers, and streetwear stores such as Autonomy, Plane and Design a Space. Coburg is also a cultural wonderland with so many weird/cool shops offering everything from elaborate wedding dresses and jewellery to gift stores and afghan bazaars, you could easily spend the day shopping, people watching and eating some exquisite middle eastern cuisine along Sydney Road.

Ellen Porteus
Graphic designer & illustrator

I'm obsessed with crazy colourful palettes, surreal patterns, and clever illustrations with a sense of humour!

Incu
P.054

Julian Frost
Animator & illustrator

I'm from New Zealand and now live in Melbourne. My job involves drawing and animating silly things.

Motherbird
Creative studio

Motherbird was founded by Jack Mussett, Dan Evans and Chris Murphy in 2009. The creative studio has worked with MTV, Qantas, Nickelodeon and Mushroom Music.

Third
Drawer
Down
P.052

Dixons
Recycled
Records
P.055

Ellie Malin
Printmaker

Inspired by a love for travel and beautiful moments in life, my artworks reflect a playful approach to image making where bright colours and form construct the landscape.

Mr Kitly
P.058

Penny Min Ferguson
Designer & illustrator

Penny Min Ferguson is the human behind Min Pin, an illustration based design label specialising in jewellery, ceramics and textiles.

Allison Colpoys & Kasia Gadecki, *The Souvenir Society*

Allison Colpoys and Kasia Gadecki met at university back in the Y2K and were instantly bonded over their love for pattern, illustration, packaging and design.

Modern
Times
P.056

Guild of
Objects
P.059

Michaela Webb
Creative director, Studio Round

Michaela co-founded design studio Round. She is responsible for creatively leading the studio's diverse projects.

Lucy Folk
P.061

Mildred & Duck
Graphic design studio

Creative directors Daniel Smith and Sigiriya Brown design for print, digital and environmental media, creating solutions for a variety of sectors that communicate and connect with people.

Paul Troon
Graphic designer

Having worked at Mahon & Band, Design By Pidgeon and as senior designer at Australian skincare brand Aesop, I now run design studio Ultra with my friend Kate Rogers.

Gertrude
Street
P.060

Dinosaur
Designs
P.062

Brett Phillips
Founder & CEO, 3 Deep

By identifying the need for strategic and entrepreneurial thinkers beyond the provision of creative services, Brett has established 3 Deep as a prominent innovative business.

Camberwell
Sunday
Market
P.064

Alexandra de Boer
Graphic designer, Elenberg Fraser

Alexandra is a graphic designer specialising in publication design, typography, branding and wayfinding.

Wona Bae & Charlie Lawler, *Founders, Loose Leaf*

Loose Leaf is a botanical design studio and retail space of indoor plants and fresh cut flowers set in a beautifully converted warehouse in Melbourne.

Wunder-
kammer
P.063

St Andrews
Market
P.065

25 Third Drawer Down
Map A, P.102

Third Drawer Down is not your typical gift store – it stocks really fun, unique, hard to find, artist-made objects, home wares, books, jewellery and a wide range of eccentric objects, which are sourced locally and internationally by their dedicated team. Its stores are independent concept destinations that curate objects in their interpretation of the traditional museum or gallery store. They also stock items produced by their design studio, which produces artist-licensed objects and bespoke ranges for cultural institutions.

🕐 Fitzroy: 1100–1700 (M–Sa),
🏠 99 George St., Fitzroy
📞 + 61 (0)3 9534 4088
URL www.thirddrawerdown.com

"*Third Drawer Down is not your typical gift shop. If you see something you like, but can't take it home with you, their online store ships internationally.*"

– Ellen Porteus

26 Incu
Map B, P.104

Nestled in bustling fashion filled Flinders Lane is Incu, the uniquely innovative brainchild of twin brothers Brian and Vincent Wu. Born out of the brothers' love of travel and international brands, and a desire to showcase upcoming Aussie talent, the fashion and lifestyle product retailer first opened their doors in 2002 and now own seven branches in Sydney and Melbourne. Incu's Flinders Lane location exclusively stocks menswear but the two stores at QV on Albert Coates Lane cater to women and men. Incu also carries their own daily wear label, Weathered.

🕐 1000-1800 (M-Th, Sa), -2000 (F), 1100-1700 (Su)
🏠 274 Flinders Ln., CBD
📞 +61 (0)3 9663 9933
URL www.incu.com

"Incu is opposite our studio, so we often find ourselves going out for a coffee and returning with a wardrobe of clothes."

– Jack Mussett, Dan Evans & Chris Murphy, Motherbird

27 Dixons Recycled Records

Map I, P.107

Dixons Recycled Records is one of the longest running second hand music stores in Australia and is renowned as a great source of bargain goods and hard to find items. With two outposts, Dixons buys and sells used LP records, CDs, vintage Hi-Fi, magazines and other collectables, next to a library of indie, punk, rock, pop, dance, metal, country, blues and experimental sounds. Anything by the following obscure Aussie bands is a winner: The Ninnies (bush folk), Mountain Maggot (punk), Born Hungry (ska-metal), Darren and the Pubes (pub rock).

🕐 Fitzroy: 0930–1800 (M-Th),
  –2100 (F), 1000– (Sa), 1100–(Su)
🏠 414 Brunswick St., Fitzroy
📞 +61 (0)3 9416 2272
URL www.dixons.com.au

"My favourite souvenir when travelling is CDs. Find an album from a popular local band c.1985 for an insight into local culture."

– Julian Frost

28 Modern Times
Map A, P.103

Modern Times is a temple of mid-century modern designs. It started out as a series of pop-up shops in 2010 but has now become a permanent fixture on the local vintage furniture scene, boasting choice vintage Danish furniture alongside locally made homewares and art specially picked to complement the style. At their fabulous big space, expect to find everything from highly collectable Danish pieces in teak and rosewood by celebrated designers such as Hans Wegner and Arne Vodder, to small gifts lovingly handcrafted by a local talents.

🕙 1000–1800 (M-F), –1700 (Sa), 1100– (Su)
🏠 311 Smith St., Fitzroy
📞 +61 (0)3 9913 8598
URL moderntimes.com.au

"Stop next door at Shop Ramen for a heart-warming noodle soup or cross the road to Alimentari for a delicious meal."

– Ellie Malin

29 **Mr Kitly**
📍 Map K, P.108

Combining a light-filled shop, gallery and architecture studio, Mr Kitly is like a secret garden tucked away in a Victorian-era building. It is particularly noted for their thoughtful and considered collection of functional objects in ceramic, wood, metal, textiles and fibres, with a strong nod to Japanese aesthetics. Run by Bree Claffey, Mr Kitly, named after their pet cat, also stocks a wide range of books related to crafts, design and architecture, as well as indoor plants. The gallery features monthly exhibitions of both local and international artists, whose artworks are often available for purchase after.

🕐 1100–1800 (M, W–Sa), –1600 (Su)
🏠 1/F, 381 Sydney Rd., Brunswick (stairs: next door to Super Cheap Fabrics)
📞 +61 (0)3 9078 7357 🔲 www.mrkitly.com.au

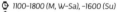

"We love this store – it will serve all of your present buying needs. Keep your eyes peeled for their sandwich board sign on the street."

– Allison Colpoys & Kasia Gadecki, The Souvenir Society

30 Guild of Objects
Map E, P.106

Affectionately known as 'Guild', Guild of Objects is a cute little store in North Melbourne run by three small batch potters. Brooke Thorn, Chela Edmunds and Tao Oudomvilay started Guild in 2015 as a way for them to share their own work and now the cute little store also exhibits the work of many other artists and makers with the local community. This place sells an amazing array of unique and beautiful one-of-a-kind ceramics, jewellery and textiles that are completely Australian made. Guild also hosts crafting workshops by local crafters too. Check their Guild Classes page for time and day.

🕐 1000–1700 (Th-Sa)
🏠 690 Queensberry St., North Melbourne
📞 +61 (0)432 647 445
URL guildofobjects.com

"This is a great place to pick up a souvenir and support the local designers. Check out Hot Poppy (9 Errol St.) for a great lunch too!"

– Penny Min Ferguson, Min Pin

31 Gertrude Street

Map A, P.102

Gertrude Street is just one of Melbourne's many shopping strips and can be found a short stroll or quick tram ride from the city in Fitzroy. The diverse street is filled with coffee shops, fashion outlets, stores, bars and restaurants and is the perfect place to make the short walk from the city to Smith Street, a very long one. Grab a coffee and arepas at Sonido to fuel up before you start shopping. Make sure you check out Bruce, Third Drawer Down (#25), bookstore TITLE, Gertrude Contemporary gallery and finish the day with a cocktail at The Everleigh.

🏠 Gertrude St., Fitzroy
🔗 cutlerandco.com.au, sonido.com.au, www.shopbruce.com.au, titlestore.com.au, www.theeverleigh.com, www.gertrude.org.au

"*Make a booking at Cutler & Co.!*"
– Michaela Webb, Studio Round

32 Lucy Folk
Map B, P.105

Lucy Folk is an Australian jewellery brand headed up by its namesake creative director and trained silversmith, Lucy Folk. A self-confessed foodie and global traveller, Folk indulges a taste for the sweet and beautiful which is reflected in a buffet of ornamental hors d'oeuvres, anchovy rings and wittily delicious gems. Folk's husband and architect Charlie Inglis has designed the flagship shop space, with custom cabinets and Folk's corn chip handles to store her enticing pieces. The designer also creates bespoke pieces and is available to meet in person at her Melbourne studio or on location during her trips.

🕙 1100–1700 (Tu–W, F), –1800 (Th), 1000–1700 (Sa)
📍 1A Crossley St., CBD
📞 +61 (0)3 9663 6829
🔗 www.lucyfolk.com

"Lucy Folk is a great place to get accessories good enough to eat. While you're there make sure you try some of the bars and cafés at Crossley Street."

– Daniel Smith & Sigiriya Brown, Mildred & Duck

33 Dinosaur Designs

Map B, P.104

Dinosaur Designs is an eclectic store packed with jewellery, homewares and lifestyle products that have been designed by Australian designers and life partners Louise Olsen and Stephen Ormandy since 1986. This talented design duo annually produces two beautifully-coloured resin jewellery and homeware collections, often inspired by nature and are truly unique. All items are lovingly and sustainably made by hand in their Sydney studio by skilled artisans under Olsen and Stephen's direction.

🕐 1000–1800 (M–Th, Sa), –2000 (F), 1100–1700 (Su) 🏠 Shop T06, The Strand Melbourne, 250 Elizabeth St., CBD ☎ +61 (0)3 9650 8000 📟 www.dinosaurdesigns.com.au

"When travelling overseas and in need of a gift to take, I always gather a few of their one-off pieces as a slice of home to share with friends around the world."

– Paul Troon, Ultra

34 Wunderkammer
Map B, P.104

Wunderkammer is one of Melbourne's shopping highlights, stocking gifts and souvenirs for people of any age and is well known for having rare and unusual items on their shelves such as antique scientific and medical instruments, fossils, framed butterflies, taxidermy, skeletons, and much more. The stores name, Wunderkammer, is derived from the German for 'Cabinet of Curiosities', which is an old concept where people take unique, odd and sometimes strange items that they have found and assemble them in wooden cabinets with glass fronted display windows.

🕐 1000-1800 (M-F), -1600 (Sa)
🏠 439 Lonsdale St., CBD
📞 +61 (0)3 9642 4694
f Wunderkammer

"Take your time to browse the rare and the unusual."
– Brett Phillips, 3 Deep

35 Camberwell Sunday Market
Map V, P.110

The Camberwell Sunday Market is a popular trash and treasure market that only sells second hand goods or hand-crafted goods, specifically made by the stallholder, excluding food. It's a great place to find vintage clothing, crockery and books as well as unusual things like photo albums, typewriters and ornaments, and you can easily put in a whole Sunday morning wandering through the marketplace on the hunt for treasures and haggling with stall owners to save a few dollars. The added bonus is that proceeds raised from the markets will benefit a number of charities.

🕐 0700-1230 (Su)
🏠 Camberwell Marketplace Car Park, Station St., Camberwell URL sundaymarket.com.au

"Make sure you get there early to experience the charm of the Camberwell Market, where treasures are endless and bargains are made to be haggled!"

– Alexandra de Boer, Elenberg Fraser

36 St Andrews Market
Map S, P.110

St Andrews Market is a vibrant and earthy Saturday market on the outskirts of Melbourne that has been part of the local community for over 40 years. It is a great place to relax and take in the bush atmosphere which has a passion for selling fresh, handmade, recycled and creative products and organic food and fresh fruit. You can also get massages, hair braiding, kids pony rides and take part in Tai Chi. There's also some delicious food stalls available and a great variety of Buskers to watch.

🕐 0800–1400 (Sa except on days of Total Fire Ban in the central)
📍 Corner Kangaroo Ground St Andrews Rd. & Proctor St., St Andrews
📞 +61 (0)467 535 341
URL standrewsmarket.com.au

"There's nothing better than sipping a chai tea on the hill overlooking the market."

– Wona Bae & Charlie Lawler, Loose Leaf

Restaurants & Cafés

Multicultural culinary options, coffee houses and modern cooking

Melbourne boasts not only being Australia's food and coffee capital but is also a global culinary hotspot, offering cuisines from all over the world that have been influenced by its rich multicultural history. The flavours of Melbourne started with the traditional indigenous owners and was gradually added to by the British settlers and the many ethnic groups that emigrated to the city following the second world war from the Netherlands, Italy and Greece. Following subsequent wars and conflicts many Yugoslavian, Turkish, Lebanese, Vietnamese and Cambodian people also migrated to Melbourne. There is also large Chinese, Indian and Sri Lankan communities to mention just a few. Each of these groups brought with them the cooking styles of their homelands resulting in a deliciously diverse mix of restaurants and cafés lining the streets and suburbs of Melbourne. Most recently many Ethiopian restaurants, such as Abesha, opened up in Footscray, and there is also a strip of Italian restaurants along Lygon Street in Carlton, dumpling and chinese restaurants in China-town and Box Hill and Vietnamese restaurants along Victor Street in Abbotsford. Melburnians also love going out to catch up with friends for weekend brunch at places like SOJO (#40), Monk Bodhi Dharma (#46) and Auction Rooms (#45) and are also passionate about coffee, which we can also thank Melbourne's multicultural past for. The coffee culture can be experienced throughout Melbourne and local baristas are so dedicated to coffee that Melbourne is regularly voted as one of the world's best coffee destinations.

Bardo
Design collaborative

Bardo is the collaborative experience of Bren Imboden and Luis Viale. They work with agencies, institutions, cultural events, start-ups and established companies worldwide.

The Town Mouse
P.071

Surya Prasetya
Founder & director, Studio SP-GD

At Studio SP-GD, we develop ideas and offer creative direction, branding and identity for various industries. In my spare time I enjoy designing and making furniture and objects.

UNA
Creative studio

Founded by Andrew Archer and Kelly Thompson, UNA helps brands, individuals and agencies to connect with consumers and solve marketing problems with stunning visuals.

The Independent
P.070

SUPER-RANDOM
P.072

Christopher Boots
Industrial designer

I run a humble studio focusing on creating beautiful, timeless lighting sculptures. I'm inspired and driven by nature – crystals and quantum concepts are always on my mind.

Grub Food Van
P.074

Charlie Romeo Brophy
Photographer

I'm really just a tomboyish girl born in a concrete jungle, fulfilling a creative vision through photography and exploring mother nature in other parts of the world.

Livia Arena
Creative director, Livia Arena

I'm Livia Arena, creative director of the eponymous Australian women's fashion label. Established in 2011, Livia Arena's designs focus on relaxed styling with luxury finishes.

South of Johnston
P.073

Carolina Café & Bar
P.076

Billie Justice Thomson
Painter & illustrator

I specialise in reverse glass painting and have painted the windows of many shops in and around Melbourne. I particularly love food and nostalgic food imagery in my projects.

Mina-no-ie
P.078

Dom Bartolo & Ryan Guppy, *Founders, 21–19*

21–19 is a communications agency in Collingwood, Melbourne. We have been building stories that reach audiences, touch hearts and influence minds since 2005.

Half Moon Café
P.077

Jack Vanzet
Creative director & musician

I'm a 24 year old creative director and musician from Melbourne.

Auction Rooms
P.080

Glenn Thomas
Illustrator

Glenn Thomas is an illustrator working under the alias The Fox And King. He is currently working on several commercial and personal projects.

Monk Bodhi Dharma
P.081

Cumulus Up
P.082

Alex & Tim Britten-Finschi, *FROM BRITTEN P/L*

The founders of the international Menswear brand have lived in Melbourne all their lives. They travel for work and for the best food in every country they visit.

Fabio Ongarato
Founder, Fabio Ongarato Design

Fabio Ongarato Design is a multidisciplinary design studio. Their work is built on creative collaboration, strategic thinking and a holistic approach to design.

Supernormal
P.083

37 The Independent
Map W, P.110

The Independent is beautifully positioned in the Dandenong Ranges on Melbourne's outskirts. High ceiling, extensive floor area, exposed timber and white-painted bricks, the restaurant has maintained a rustic charm of the former hardware store, which is softened by a herb-filled beer garden complete with kids' play area. Inspired by the seasons, the day's fresh ingredients and chef Mauro Callegari's Argentinian roots, dishes here are designed for the whole table to enjoy. A Morcilla – crumbed black pudding with chickpeas and tomatoes comes in as smaller portions, whereas the crispy spiced chicken breast is more filling.

🕐 1200 till late (W–Su)
🏠 79 Main St., Gembrook
📞 +61 (0)3 5968 1110
🔗 www.theindependentgembrook.com.au

"Don't miss the Provoleta. It's one of our favourite dishes – baked cheese with chimichurri."

– Bren Imboden & Luis Viale, Bardo

38 The Town Mouse

Map A, P.102

The Town Mouse is a neighbourhood restaurant and bar with fine eats and a diverse selection of biodynamic wines, delectable cocktails and liquor. Its Art Deco interior is fitted with black tiles, raw wooden stools and vintage glass lamp shades. Despite the metal braced bar area centring the space, meticulously prepared dishes are still the essential experience at The Town Mouse. Do ask the friendly crew for more recommendations on top of the scrumptious oyster with chardonnay vinegar sorbet or the aromatic Lamb flank with courgette and pistachio.

🕒 1800–0000 (M, Th), 1200– (F–Su)
🏠 312 Drummond St., Carlton
☎ +61 (0)3 9347 3312
🌐 www.thetownmouse.com.au

"Trust the staff to suggest a wine match, they always manage to impress and cater well no matter what your tastes."

– Andrew Archer & Kelly Thompson, UNA

39

SUPERRANDOM
Map M, P.108

SUPERRANDOM is a small café in Brighton much-loved by the neighbourhood for its great coffee. Its menu only carries one blend (simply called 'coffee') and simple food one can have on-the-go such as baguettes and muffins. If you are not in a rush, have a seat in one of their eclectic mix of old chairs, have a delicious pressed jaffle sandwich on the cement block tables and enjoy the simplicity of the city's hidden gem.

🏠 *416 New St., Brighton*
📞 *+61 (0)3 9596 0990*

"*Nobu is an award winning Japanese barista and makes the best coffee on the south-side. Make sure you order a Jaffle with your coffee.*"
– Surya Prasetya, Studio SP-GD

40 South of Johnston
Map A, P.103

South of Johnston is an old valve-repackaging factory that has been completely transformed merging modern style and sustainability with a charming, country vista. Fruit trees have been planted in wooden crates out the front that will grow into an urban orchard that locals are encouraged to pick as they pass, while the thoughtful inclusion of various rural knick knacks, old farming tools and a European open fire place ensure the influence never goes over-board. SOJO's seasonal lunch menu caters for a variety of tastes and dietary requirements.

🕐 0730–1700 (M-Su)
🏠 46 Oxford St., Collingwood
📞 +61 (0)3 9417 2741
📘 South of Johnston

"An excellent example of Melbourne's gastronomical options. Come early (before 10am) on the weekends if you don't want to wait too long!"

– Christopher Boots

41 Grub Food Van

Map A, P.102

Grub Food Van is a low key cafe, which features a 1965 Airstream van in the yard of the owners' house. The tables and chairs scattered around outside the van are the perfect spot to enjoy on a clear morning or warm sunny day. On cold days you can stay warm, and dry, in the greenhouse. The cafe uses some of the produce they grow in the greenhouse below their home for their simple menu of all-day snacks such as sandwiches, panini and 'boards' with a selection of cheeses, terrines and fresh produce.

🕐 0800–2100 (Tu–Sa), –1700 (Su)
🏠 87-89 Moor St., Fitzroy
📞 +61 (0)3 9419 8991
URL www.grubfoodvan.com.au

"Make friends with the dog, and make sure you use the bathrooms and have a listen to their amazing radio documentary soundtrack."

– Livia Arena

42 Carolina Café & Bar
Map F, P.106

Carolina is a café by day and a bar by night with an impressive list of cocktails, boutique beers and ciders and a tasty bar menu. Housed in an old shoemaker's shop, it is complemented by a beautiful leafy courtyard – the perfect setting for a lazy afternoon in the sun. Food is served until 3pm, which mainly consists of breakfasts and light meals that go well with coffee from local roaster Industry Beans. It is hard to choose from a classic Monte Cristo sandwich or a Lambwich – slow-braised lamb shoulder with baba ghanoush, wild rocket, green olive salsa and smoked paprika.

🕐 0800–1600 (M–F), 0830– (Sa–Su)
🏠 11 Nicholson St., Brunswick East
📞 +61 (0)425 731 315
f Carolina Cafe & Bar

"The light in the intimate courtyard falls beautifully and feels like someone has opened up their backyard to you for brunch."

– Charlie Romeo Brophy

43 Half Moon Café

Map J, P.108

A short trip north of the CBD on the number eight tram leads you to Coburg, which is a cultural wonderland of weird and wonderful stores, bars and restaurants. It is also home to a lot of Middle Eastern restaurants, such as Half Moon Café which has earned a cult following with many locals for their delicious falafels that are made in the Egyptian style using broad beans instead of chickpeas. The courtyard is a great place to sit and watch the diverse mix of people pass by before you explore this interesting suburb.

🕘 0900–1700 daily
🏠 13 Victoria St., Coburg
📞 +61 (0)3 9350 2949

"They have the most delicious falafel I've ever eaten – so fluffy and the pickles are amazing. Explore the neighbourhood! Coburg is a cultural wonderland with many cool shops."

– Billie Justice Thomson

44 Mina·no·ie

Map A, P.103

Mina·no·ie is a Japanese cafe slightly off the beat of Smith Street in an old industrial warehouse. The space's heritage has been maintained with long communal tables, mismatched chairs, stools and benches coupled with hanging plants and industrial lighting. The menu is filled with a selection of organic Japanese home style dishes that stay true to Mina·no·ie's philosophy of providing sustenance with a balance of flavours. The café also shares the space with their in-store shop CIBI, which carries a range of artisan Japanese homewares, ceramics, textiles and books that will make the perfect souvenir.

🕐 0800-1600 (Tu-F), 0900- (Sa)
🏠 33 Peel St., Collingwood
📞 +61 (0)3 9417 7749
🔗 minanoie.com

"This is our local eatery and coffee shop. It is our home away from home – be sure to say hello to us if you see us in there."

– Dom Bartolo & Ryan Guppy, 21-19

45 Auction Rooms
Map E, P.106

Auction Rooms, sits conveniently in the heart of old North Melbourne, which has been gentrified but still emits a heritage charm. Housed in the old WB Ellis Auction House, it provides a reasonably priced and creative brunch menu, which it has become renowned for. The coffee is also worth a trip to North Melbourne – they roast specialty blends onsite in their enormous red coffee roaster, which adds to the charm of the chic industrial interior. An entire wall is filled with a selection of beans that you can buy for brewing at home.

🕐 0700–1700 (M–F), 0730– (Sa–Su)
🏠 103–107 Errol St., North Melbourne
📞 +61 (0)3 9326 7749
URL www.auctionroomscafe.com.au

"Make sure you go for a stroll around the back streets of North Melbourne to check out some of the old heritage buildings."

– Jack Vanzet

46 Monk Bodhi Dharma
Map Q, P.109

Monk Bodhi Dharma is tucked away behind
Carlisle Street and looks unassuming from
the street but is impressive once inside. It is
a specialist coffee and tea house that stocks
a range of healing teas to get you regrouped
and rebalanced and is completely vegetarian – you won't even find eggs on the menu.
The humble interior is a blend of aged wood,
worn brick and neat tiles filled with communal
restored workbenches and vintage Singer
sewing tables. On Friday evenings they also do
vegetarian and raw dinners – with seatings at
6.30 and 8.30pm.

🕐 *0700–1700 (M–F), 0800– (Sa–Su)*
🏠 *Rear 202 Carlisle St., Balaclava*
📞 *+61 (0)3 9534 7250*
🔗 *www.monkbodhidharma.com*

"This hidden gem's house roasted coffee is
undeniably the best in Melbourne. Try the Sweetcorn
Hotcakes – they are amazing."
– Glenn Thomas aka The Fox And King

47 Cumulus Up
Map B, P.105

Cumulus Up is a city loft wine bar with a delicious food menu served in an elegant and warm interior. The space features parquet timber floors, blown glass pendant lights, marble tables, steel features exposed bricks and wall mirrors, which all blend together nicely to create a stunning effect. The menu with its grilled seafood, dry aged beef, roast Holmbrae chicken and a selection of cheeses, to mention just a few tasty treats, has been designed to complement the impressive and eclectic wine list, which is housed onsite in their climate controlled cellar.

⏰ 1700–0000 (Su–Th), 1600–0100 (F–Su)
🏠 45 Flinders Ln., CBD
📞 +61 (0)3 9650 1445
URL www.cumulusinc.com.au/up

"The food and drinks are an exceptional quality that foodies will love. If the duck waffles with foie gras are on the menu, it's a must try."

– Alex & Tim Britten-Finschi, FROM BRITTEN P/L

48 Supernormal

Map B, P.105

Supernormal is an Asian influenced canteen on Flinders Lane with an understated fit out that feels Japanese with its large open plan kitchen, Japanese snack vending machines and basement karaoke room. The menu takes you on a journey through Asia with many Chinese inspired dishes on the menu such as dumplings, slow-cooked peppery lamb and cold cut chicken with noodles, it also has many Korean and Japanese influenced dishes, ingredients and flavours that you can wash down with one of their impressive cocktails. The dessert menu is delightful so make sure you save some room.

🕐 1100–2300 (Su–Th), –0000 (F–Sa)
🏠 180 Flinders Ln., CBD
☎ +61 (0)3 9650 8688
URL supernormal.net.au

"The lobster rolls! Bookings are essential or turn up early."

– Fabio Ongarato, Fabio Ongarato Design

Nightlife

Vibrant rooftop bars, live music venues and more movies

Thousands of bars, pubs and clubs spread throughout the city's rooftops, laneways, streets and suburbs. There are a lot of different bar strips that offer something for everyone. Places like Chapel Street are a perfect example of Melbourne's vibrant and diverse nightlife where you can grab a drink at one of the small bars such as La La Land, Wonderland or Hoo Ha before dancing the night away at Revolver to one of the many big name DJs who frequently play there or listen to live music in the band room. St Kilda is nearby, which is the perfect place to grab a bite to eat at one of the restaurants along Fitzroy and Acland Streets before heading to a nearby bar or club or if live music is your thing check out the Espy (The Esplanade Hotel). Or head across the river into the city and grab a drink at Cookie, which is below The Toff in Town (#59) and Rooftop Bar and Cinema (#22). Not far from the CBD is the bustling suburb of Fitzroy where you can take in the scenery and enjoy sunset from the rooftop bar Naked in the Sky, watch some live music at The Tote (#57) or head to Sydney Road Brunswick or High Street Northcote to watch some live music in any of the live music venues along both these strips. Melbourne's nightlife is spread out so pick an area and bar hop to save spending the night in taxis or trams. Check out www.barsandnightclubs.com.au/melbourne/ before heading out to decide on which venues to hit up or www.inthemix.com.au is a great gig guide.

Georgia Perry
Graphic artist

I work with clients from around the world on illustration, graphic design and fine art projects, as well as producing my own range of products.

Jesse Gerner
Executive chef

I'm Jesse Gerner. I am the executive chef and owner of three Melbourne venues – Añada, Bomba and Green Park Dining. I live in Thornbury with my wife Vanessa and our three sons.

Kristoffer Paulsen
Photographer & musician

I'm a freelance photographer and musician originally from Sydney, but moved to Melbourne in 2007.

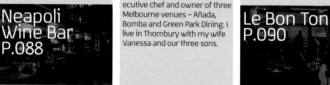

David Flack
Founder, Flack Studio

I'm an interior architect and designer. I'm always excited to discover new treasures, whether on little jaunts around our beautiful city or on regular overseas travels.

Darcy Prendergast
Founder, Oh Yeah Wow

Darcy Prendergast is an avid fan of dinosaurs, Vikings and trampolines but also dabbles in the writing and directing of music videos, short films and TV.

Glendyn Ivin
Director

Glendyn Ivin is a director of television, film and commercials. His film *Cracker Bag* won the Palme d'Or for Short Film in 2003 at the Cannes Film Festival.

Auver Austria
Creative director, AĀRK Collective

AĀRK Collective creates unisex timepieces that are inspired by an appreciation for geometric form, graphic elements and timeless design.

LongPlay
P.096

Some Velvet
Morning
P.097

Travis Aulsebrook
Musician

Travis Aulsebrook aka Hudson & Troop is a future-folk musician living in the Brunswick East suburb. He has released two EP's and a string of singles, including *The Dream* in 2015.

Tajette O'Halloran
Photographer

I'm constantly finding my way and exploring new ideas in photography. I am drawn to the discomposed human experience where I am often the subject of my own work.

The Tote
P.098

Ben Thomas
Photographer & visual artist

I'm a photographer, author, brewer and public Wi-Fi and smart city geek based in Melbourne. I have recently released my first book, *Tiny Tokyo: The Big City Made Mini*.

Horse
Bazaar
P.099

The Toff in
Town
P.100

Chela
Musician & producer

I am Chelsea May, a musician/producer/performer/artist/filmmaker. I release singles as Chela, including *Romanticise* and *Zero* on Kitsune in Paris, and *Handful of Gold* on iHeartComix in LA.

Confetti Studio
Design studio

We are Tom Shanahan and Kevin McDowell and we head the multidisciplinary design studio, Confetti. Together we are also one half of wonky hypno-disco band, Mildlife.

Hugs &
Kisses
P.101

49 Neapoli Wine Bar
Map B, P.104

Neapoli Wine Bar is a sleek, masculine yet elegant space. The interior is decked out with amber wood, polished concrete and stainless steel, with a sweeping wrought iron staircase that takes you up to the mezzanine, which has been lined with American Oak and is the perfect place for an intimate meal. The floor to ceiling front window perfectly frames the alley and outdoor terrace seating. The menu is filled with a mix of comfort foods, sandwiches and a delicious sharing menu perfect to be washed down by one of the many wines from their cellar.

🕐 0700 till late (M–F), 0800 till late (Sa–Su)
🏠 30 Russell Place, CBD
📞 +61 (0)3 9650 5020
URL www.neapoliwinebar.com.au

"Beautiful fit-out, great service and delicious food and drinks! It's the perfect place for a Friday knock-off drink (or three)."

– Georgia Perry

50 Bomba
Map B, P.105

While Bomba is one of many Melbourne rooftop bars, this one is extra special. It is inspired by the modern bodega and has an intimate fit out. The red-hued room has festooned, woven straw light shades, a retractable roof and views across the skyline and rooftops. The tapas menu is inspired by the chefs' Spanish roots and the delicious simple and affordable treats can be washed down by one of the many killer cocktails on their list.

🕐 1200–1500, 1700–0100 (M–F), 1700–0100 (Sa–Su)
🏠 Level 5, 103 Lonsdale St., CBD
📞 +61 (0)3 9077 0451
🌐 www.bombabar.com.au

"*Melburnians particularly love rooftop spaces with enough brilliant rooftops to keep you busy all week.*"

– Jesse Gerner, Añada, Bomba & Green Park Dining

51 **Le Bon Ton**
Map A, P.103

Le Bon Ton is a late night bar and supper club tucked away in Collingwood. This Southern American smokehouse, absinthe salon, cocktail bar and oyster room is a tribute to the Big Easy and is based around the culture, music, food and decor of the old houses in New Orleans. Le Bon Ton has a relaxed atmosphere to chill out in and enjoy some southern food or sample some of their extensive range of Absinthe. They don't stop serving smoked meats until 5am and last drinks is 6am.

🕐 1700–0100 (M), 1200–0100 (Tu–Th), –0600 (F–Sa), –0000 (Su)
🏠 51 Gipps St., Collingwood
📞 +61 (0)3 9416 4341
URL www.Lebonton.com.au

"A wild Louisiana style saloon serving up cocktails, chilli cheese fries that are addictive, smoked meat and rocking out till 6am."
– Kristoffer Paulsen

 52 Neighbourhood Wine
Map F, P.106

Neighbourhood Wine is an excellent bistro that serves seasonal French style rustic food coupled with wines from every corner of the world in a dim and moody setting. The cosy wooden tables, long wide candle lit bar and rows of 60s and 70s jazz and blues records that play on high rotation make for the perfect setting for a romantic dinner or drink. It also has a super fascinating back-story as an illegal casino and hangout for Melbourne underworld in the late 1980s. A lot of the original decor remains after a police raid shut it down 25 years before the new owner discovered it.

🕐 1200-0000 daily
🏠 1 Reid St., Fitzroy North
📞 +61 (0)3 9486 8306
URL www.neighbourhoodwine.com

"Stay late after dinner, have a game of billiards in the Sunset Club, then ask your waiter to show the secret compartment."

– David Flack, Flack Studio

53 Forgotten Worlds
Map A, P.103

Forgotten Worlds seamlessly blends drinking with arcade games. The entry is filled with a clutter of vintage arcade games and retro furniture. You'll find all the old classic video games inside – Double Dragon, Mortal Kombat, Street Fighter, The Simpsons, Virtua Cop...the list goes on – and the best part is they still cost the same as they did back in the day. The bar specialises in beer, and their preference is to serve them canned, of which they have an impressive list of more than 70 beers form around the country. If you want to escape the arcade games there's street front seating or a minimalist courtyard filled with hanging plants and a shed.

🕐 1600–2300 (W–Th), –0100 (F–Sa), –2300 (Su)
🏠 113 Johnston St., Collingwood
📞 +61 (0)3 9416 4080
📘 Forgotten Worlds

"It's genius really and impossible to have a bad time. Watch out for the 'penis robots' in Michael Jackson's classic 'Moonwalker'... They're tricky."

– Darcy Prendergast, Oh Yeah Wow

54 Kustom Kommune
Map A, P.103

The Kustom Kommune is a unique warehouse space tucked away in the backstreets of Collingwood that combines beers with motorbikes and slow cooked meat to make for an unforgettable experience. It started as Australia's first communal motorcycle workshop/garage and a community space but then also grew into a weekend bar and Texan BBQ joint that on Friday, Saturday and Sunday nights serves meats that are sourced from local farmers and smoked onsite for 12 hours in a wood fired smoker. The drink offering changes each week so check out their facebook page for updates.

🕐 1000–2100 (Tu–Th), –0000 (F–Su)
🏠 25 Easy St., Collingwood
📞 +61 (0)3 9417 5123
URL kustomkommune.com.au

"Easily Melbourne's coolest bar. Great atmosphere, awesome people and amazing energy. Get in early to avoid the queues."

– Glendyn Ivin

55 LongPlay
Map F, P.106

LongPlay is a low key bar set in a converted shop front with a small but satisfying menu and a private cinema space providing a contrasting experience to that of traditional cinema houses. The warm, cosy and inviting interior has a nice mix of Danish furnishings and is a blend between an American diner and an old Italian bistro. The wine, beer and cider list is nicely selected but their cocktail list is exceptional – it contains all the old classics and won't cost you a fortune either.

🕐 1800–2300 (Su–W), –0100 (Th–Sa)
🏠 318 St Georges Rd., Fitzroy North
📞 +61 (0)400 155 891
🔗 www.longplay.net.au

"Organise a screening of a movie of your choice with friends (maximum 30 people). It's an intimate and memorable way to watch a film together."

– Auver Austria, AĀRK Collective

56 Some Velvet Morning
Map O, P.109

Some Velvet Morning is one of Melbourne's smallest live music venues but what it lacks in size it makes up for in entertainment. This bar books some of the best acts in Melbourne, which play five nights a week and they also holds regular piano karaoke and Bluegrass Bingo nights on Tuesdays and Wednesdays, respectively. The backroom is fit out like someone's grandma's living room and the ingredients on the breakfast, lunch and dinner menus is all as locally sourced as possible.

🕐 0800–2300 (Tu–W), –0100 (Th–Su), 0900–2200 (Su)
🏠 123 Queens Parade, Clifton Hill
📞 +61 (0)3 9486 5192
URL www.somevelvetmorning.com.au

"Owned by musicians and the friendliest bunch of people, this place books the best local music. Try the nachos, they're top notch."

– Travis Aulsebrook aka Hudson & Troop

57 The Tote

Map A, P.103

The Tote is one of Melbourne's favourite live rock and roll venues. This institution is so loved that 20,000 people marched in 2010 protesting to save it from closure. The march was a success and the strict licensing laws that threatened many venues like The Tote were changed. The band room is often packed when gigs are on, which is most nights, so be sure to arrive early to secure your spot. There's also a large courtyard to cool off when you need a break from dancing and if you want to listen to any of your favourite songs head to the front bar and take control of the jukebox.

🕐 1600-0100 (W), -0300 (Th-Sa), -2300 (Su)
🏠 71 Johnston St., Collingwood
📞 +61 (0)3 9419 5320
URL www.thetotehotel.com

"Yay! It's dirty. It's loud. The carpet is sticky as hell but there's no other place like it. Drink responsibly."

– Tajette O'Halloran

58 Horse Bazaar
Map B, P.104

Neatly tucked away on Little Lonsdale street in Melbourne's CBD is Horse Bazaar, which is a Japanese influenced bar that fuses visual arts with live music, speciality drinks and 'Izakaya' inspired soul food. Horse Bazaar has long been a hub for digital arts and when you experience their 20-metre continuous digital canvas, which new media and digital artworks are projected, you'll understand why. The extensive bottled beer menu offers 40 odd beers from every continent of the world, there's four beers on tap and a wide ranging cocktail menu.

🕐 1600-0000 (M-Tu), 1200- (W-Th), 1200 till late (F), 1700- (Sa)
🏠 397 Little Lonsdale St., CBD
☎ +61 (0)3 9670 2329
URL www.horsebazaar.com.au

"There's a showcase of some of the best hip hop and beats to be found in Melbourne, teamed up with the craziest projection setups I've seen."
– Ben Thomas

59 The Toff in Town
Map B, P.104

The Toff in Town is an iconic Melbourne venue that hosts some of Melbourne (and beyond)'s greatest musical artists and comedians. It's split into a few sections – the band room, the main bar, which is dominated by a number of train carriage-like booths that allow for something of a private gathering. If you manage to snag one of these coveted spots, ring for service to order some food or cocktails. There are also two outdoor areas – a spacious area at the back of the bar and a not so spacious front balcony that faces Swanston Street.

🕑 1830–2230 (F-Su), 1130–1430 (Sa-Su, Oct-Feb)
🏠 Level 2, Curtin Hse., 252 Swanston St., CBD
📞 +61 (0)3 9639 8770
URL www.thetoffintown.com

"Look up the band room schedule online so you can head there on a night in which you can discover one of your new favourite bands."
– Chela

60 Hugs & Kisses
Map B, P.104

Hugs and Kisses is a decadent members only club that knows how to throw a good party. The decks are often belting out tracks by some of Melbourne's best underground DJs and the stage frequently has a local jazz band smashing out tunes. The interior can best be described as decadent with an affinity for the absurd. You can become a member before arriving by filling out the form on their website and their facebook page has a list of all events.

🏠 *22 Sutherland St., CBD*
URL *Registrater: hugsandkisses.club/new-member*

"Newcomers are welcome with open arms. Just be sure to sign up on their website. Stay hydrated."
– Tom Shanahan & Kevin McDowell, Confetti Studio

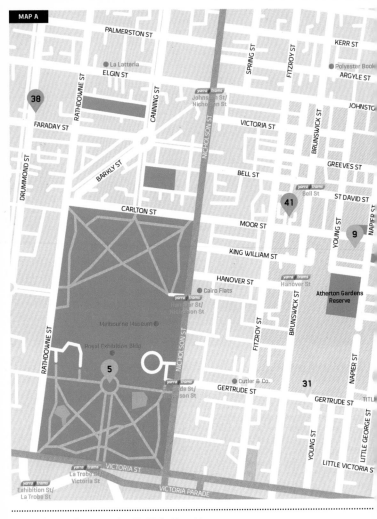

MAP A

- 5_Carlton Gardens & Royal Exhibition Building
- 9_Fitzroy backstreets
- 25_Third Drawer Down
- 38_The Town Mouse
- 41_Grub Food Van

- 19_Lamington Drive
- 20_BUS Projects
- 28_Modern Times
- 31_Gertrude Street
- 40_South of Johnston
- 44_Mina·no·ie
- 51_Le Bon Ton
- 53_Forgotten Worlds
- 54_Kustom Kommune
- 57_The Tote

MAP B

- 6_Manchester Unity Building
- 10_Nicholas Building
- 17_Daine Singer
- 21_Bennetts Lane Jazz Club
- 22_Rooftop Cinema
- 26_Incu
- 33_Dinosaur Designs
- 34_Wunderkammer
- 49_Neapoli Wine Bar
- 58_Horse Bazaar
- 59_The Toff in Town
- 60_Hugs & Kisses

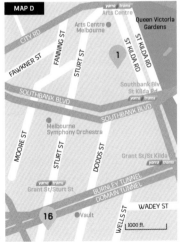

- ● 1_NGV International
- ● 3_Federation Square
- ● 4_Melbourne Cricket Ground
- ● 7_Forum Melbourne
- ● 16_ACCA
- ● 18_Craft Victoria
- ● 32_Lucy Folk
- ● 47_Cumulus Up
- ● 48_Supernormal
- ● 50_Bomba
- ★ Bennetts Lane Jazz Club (expected June 2016)

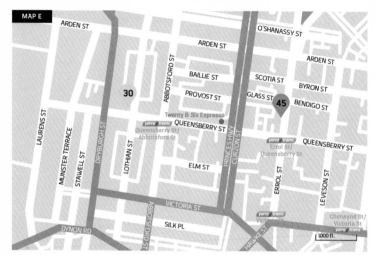

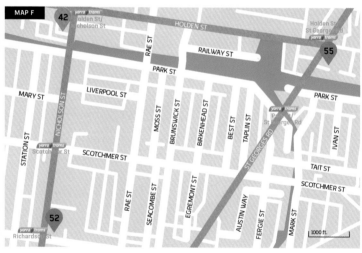

- 30_Guild of Objects
- 42_Carolina Café & Bar
- 45_Auction Rooms
- 52_Neighbourhood Wine
- 55_LongPlay

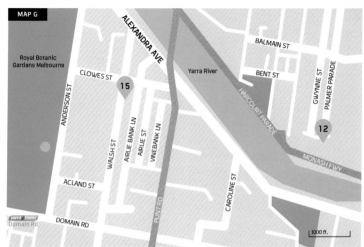

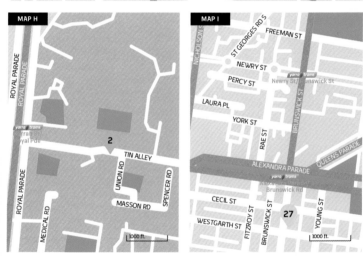

- 2_University of Melbourne
- 12_ Our Magic Hour
- 15_Robin Boyd Foundation
- 27_Dixons Recycled Records

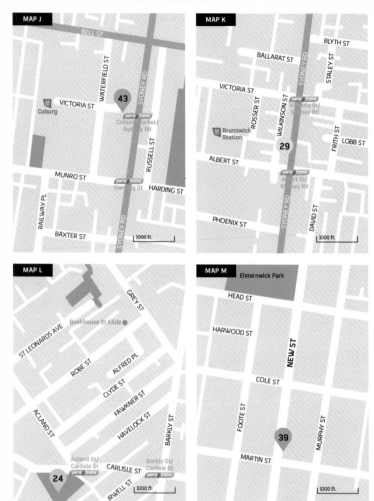

- 24_St Kilda Twilight Market
- 29_Mr Kitly
- 39_SUPERRANDOM
- 43_Half Moon Café

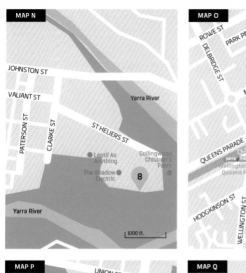

- 8_Abbotsford Convent
- 23_The Astor Theatre
- 46_Monk Bodhi Dharma
- 56_Some Velvet Morning

DISTRICT MAPS : **DOCKLANDS, ST ANDREWS, BULLEEN, KEW, CAMBERWELL, GEMBROOK**

MAP R

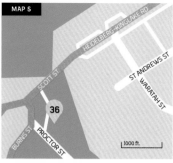

MAP S

MAP T

MAP U

MAP V

MAP W

- 11_Moonee Ponds Creek Trail
- 13_Heide Museum of Modern Art
- 14_Lyon Housemuseum
- 35_Camberwell Sunday Market
- 36_St Andrews Market
- 37_The Independent

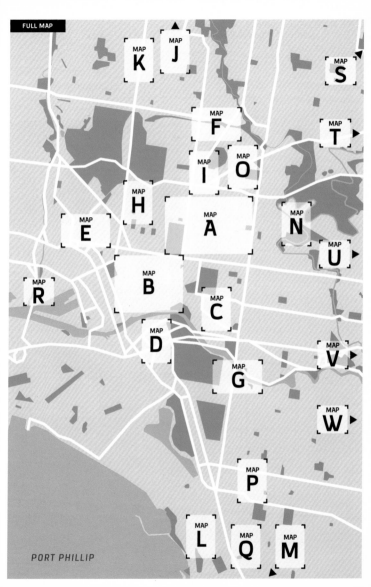

FULL MAP

PORT PHILLIP

111

Accommodation

Hip hostels, fully-equipped apartments & swanky hotels

No journey is perfect without a good night's sleep to recharge. Whether you're backpacking or on a business trip, our picks combine top quality and convenience, whatever your budget.

 < $150 $151–250 $251+

Adelphi Hotel

Recently undergone a makeover with a dessert theme, Adelphi offers 34 boldly-patterned rooms complemented by signature 1938 warehouse features. All-inclusive pricing covers welcome drink at the bar, unlimited latest-release movies, and WiFi. Be one of the first to enjoy its glass-bottomed rooftop pool that reopens in 2016.

🏠 187 Flinders Ln., CBD
📞 +61 (0)3 8080 8888
URL www.adelphi.com.au

Coppersmith

A stone's throw from Albert Park Lake lies Coppersmith, a boutique hotel with a bistro, bar and rooftop retreat. Serving only 15 guest rooms, the hotel guarantees to personalise your stay. Melbourne Sports and Aquatic Centre nearby offers world-class sporting facilities at a minimal price.

🏠 435 Clarendon St., South Melbourne
📞 +61 (0)3 8696 7777
URL coppersmithhotel.com.au

Crown Metropol

🏠 8 Whiteman St., Southbank
☎ +61 (0)3 9292 8888
URL www.crownhotels.com.au

The Prince

🏠 2 Acland St., St Kilda
☎ +61 (0)3 9536 1111
URL theprince.com.au

Hotel Lindrum Melbourne

🏠 26 Flinders St., CBD
📞 +61 (0)3 9668 1111
URL www.hotellindrum.com.au

Middle Park Hotel

🏠 102 Canterbury Rd., Middle Park
📞 +61 (0)3 9690 1958
URL middleparkhotel.com.au

Pensione Hotel Melbourne

🏠 16 Spencer St., CBD
📞 +61 (0)3 9621 3333
URL www.pensione.com.au

Notes

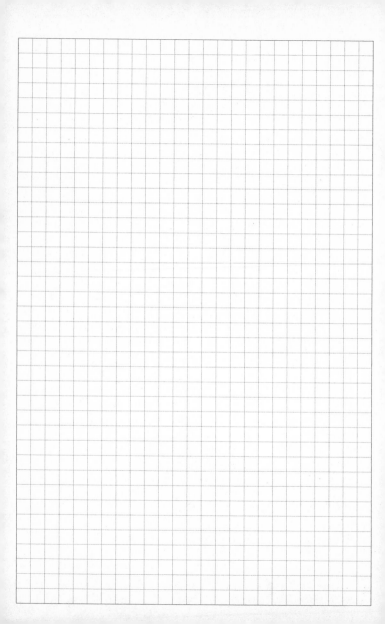

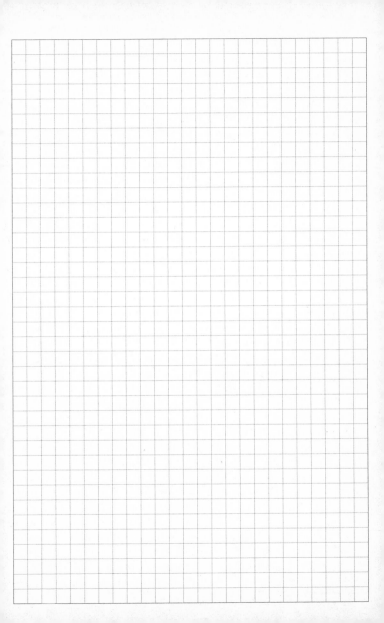

Index

Industrial

Music

Photography

Photo & other credits

—

*In Accommodation: all courtesy
of respective hotels.*

CITIX60

CITIx60: Melbourne

First published and distributed by
viction workshop ltd

viction:ary™

7C Seabright Plaza, 9-23 Shell Street,
North Point, Hong Kong

Url: www.victionary.com
Email: we@victionary.com
🅵 www.facebook.com/victionworkshop
🐦 www.twitter.com/victionary_
🐾 www.weibo.com/victionary

Edited and produced by viction:ary

Concept & art direction: Victor Cheung
Research & editorial: Queenie Ho, Caroline Kong
Project coordination: Jovan Lip, Katherine Wong
Design & map illustration: Frank Lo, MW Wong

Contributing writer: Trent Carslake
Cover map illustration: Ellen Porteus
Count to 10 illustrations: Guillaume Kashima aka Funny Fun
Photography: Daniel Aulsebrook

Content is compiled based on facts available as of August 2015. Travellers are
advised to check for updates from respective locations before your visit.

First edition
ISBN 978-988-13204-3-8
Printed and bound in China

Acknowledgements

A special thank you to all creatives, photographer(s), editor, producers, companies and organisations for your crucial contributions to our inspiration and
knowledge necessary for the creation of this book. And, to the many whose
names are not credited but have participated in the completion of the book,
we thank you for your input and continuous support all along.

City Guides

CITIx60 is a handpicked list of hot spots that illustrates the spirit of the world's most exhilarating design hubs. From what you see to where you stay, this city guide series leads you to experience the best — the places that only passionate insiders know and go.

Each volume is a unique collaboration with local creatives from selected cities. Known for their accomplishments in fields as varied as advertising, architecture and graphics, fashion, industry and food, music and publishing, these locals are at the cutting edge of what's on and when. Whether it's a one-day stopover or a longer trip, **CITIx60** is your inspirational guide.

Stay tuned for new editions.

City guides available now:

Amsterdam
Barcelona
Berlin
Hong Kong
London
Los Angeles
Melbourne
New York
Paris
Stockholm
Tokyo
Vienna